16,95

HOCKEY
THE BASICS

DAVID AND PATRICIA ARMENTROUT

The Rourke Press, Inc.
Vero Beach, Florida 32964

Patricia and David Armentrout specialize in nonfiction writing and have had several book series published for primary schools. They reside in Cincinnati with their two children.

PROJECT EDITORS:
Dick Doughty is a former Elementary School teacher who now operates his own business. He coached hockey for 9 years from the minor level through Junior "A." Dick is a certified Level 3 OMHA referee and is currently Referee-in-Chief for his hometown minor hockey association.

Rob Purdy has been a Secondary School teacher for 16 years. He is a certified Advance I hockey coach and a NCCP coaching instructor. Rob has coached hockey for 10 years in the OMHA, with a Pee Wee championship in 1997.

PHOTO CREDITS:
All photos © Kim Karpeles except © East Coast Studios: page 4;
© Mike Powell/Allsport: cover; © Gray Mortimore/Allsport: page 26

EDITORIAL SERVICES:
Penworthy Learning Systems

Library of Congress Cataloging-in-Publication Data

Armentrout, David, 1962-
    Hockey—the basics / David Armentrout, Patricia Armentrout.
        p. cm. — (Hockey)
    Includes index.
    Summary: Presents the basics of the game of hockey, including information about offensive plays such as the face-off and power play, as well as defensive plays and the role of the goalie.
    ISBN 1-57103-219-3
    1. Hockey—Juvenile literature. [1. Hockey.]   I. Armentrout, Patricia, 1960-
II. Title.   III. Series: Armentrout, David, 1962-   Hockey.
QV847.25.A756 1998
796.962—dc21   98–27532
                                                                        CIP
                                                                        AC

Printed in the USA

TABLE OF CONTENTS

BREAKOUT OPTION PASS TO THE CENTER

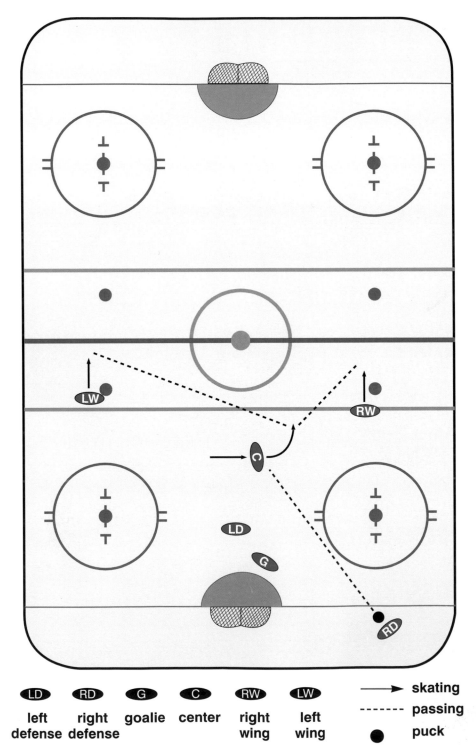

LD	RD	G	C	RW	LW
left defense	right defense	goalie	center	right wing	left wing

→ skating

----- passing

● puck

STICKHANDLING AND PASSING

As you begin playing the game of hockey, you spend a lot of time learning how to use the stick. The hockey stick is a tool—an addition to your arm. You use the stick to carry the puck, pass the puck, steal the puck, and shoot the puck. The stick is an important part of the game.

The stick has a **blade** at the bottom. Blades that curve to the left are for right-handed players. Blades that curve to the right are for left-handed players. Young, new players usually play with a stick with very little curve in the blade.

You should try out different sticks before choosing one. The stick you choose will depend on your playing style and what feels comfortable to you.

Stickhandling

Stickhandling is using a hockey stick to guide the puck along the ice. Stickhandling is sometimes necessary, but it should be avoided when possible. Passing the puck to an open teammate gets the puck up the ice much more quickly than stickhandling. Stickhandling near your own goal is not approved by most coaches, because a slip-up can easily leave the puck open for a shot on goal by an **opponent**.

Basic stickhandling rules start with hand and arm positioning. Place your hands on the **shaft** of the stick. The top hand guides and controls the stick. The bottom hand is your shooting hand. It moves up and down the shaft and gives power and direction to your shots.

Your arms should be away from your body when stickhandling. If not, the puck will end up too close to your skates and will be hard to control. It will also force you to look down at the puck instead of keeping your head up and focused on your next move.

★ **DID YOU KNOW?**

Most hockey sticks are wooden and covered in fiberglass. Some sticks have shafts made of stronger materials, like graphite and aluminum. These sticks cost more but last longer.

Sticks are made with right- or left-curved blades.

A coach demonstrates the proper grip.

Side-to-side is the most basic stickhandling technique. It is the first technique a new player should learn. Side-to-side stickhandling is going from the curve side (inside) of the blade, to the back side (outside), to push and move the puck up the ice. When you practice, keep the puck centered on the blade as you move it back and forth. Push the puck several inches each time you switch blade sides. Turn the blade each time so it partly covers the puck, to keep the puck from bouncing.

Forward-to-back is another useful stickhandling technique, but much harder to do than side-to-side. Forward-to-back works just like side-to-side, except you keep the puck beside you rather than out in front. An advantage of forward-to-back is that you are always in a passing or shooting position.

★ **COACH'S CORNER**

Keep a relaxed grip on the stick as you receive a pass. A loose grip lets you adjust more quickly to the puck's impact than a tight grip.

Passing

Passing the puck is an important part of hockey and it should be practiced as much as stickhandling and shooting. Passing involves two players: a passer and a receiver. A good pass can be lost if the receiver is not paying attention, just as a poor pass can be saved by an alert teammate.

The forehand pass, or sweep pass, is the best pass when a player has time to set it up. The forehand pass starts with a sweeping motion of the stick. As the passer, you should look at your target (the receiver's stick blade) and follow through with the stick. Your follow-through should be low and directed toward your target. As a pass receiver, hold the stick blade out in front to receive the puck. Form a wedge over the puck with the blade.

Good stickhandling and passing skills require lots of practice.

Players take turns passing the puck.

Another pass is the snap pass. Start a snap pass with the stick blade about a foot (1/3 meter) behind the puck. With a quick snap, or flick, of your wrist, hit the puck with the center of the blade. As you continue your stroke, the puck will travel forward and should snap.

A third type of pass is called the flip pass. The idea of the flip pass is to lift the puck off the ice and over an opponent or an opponent's stick towards a receiver. To start a flip pass, you need the puck tight against the heel (back) of the blade. Snap your wrist and follow through much higher than you would with an on-ice pass. It is key not to flick the puck. The high follow-through will help you get the blade under the puck and the puck into the air. The puck should land flat on the ice.

There are other passes you can learn as you play the game. Watch skilled hockey players and listen closely to your coach and soon you will be passing like a champion.

CHAPTER TWO

SHOOT TO SCORE

Most players enjoy making a shot on goal, but it is a rare event in a hockey game. Even a forward, whose job is to score, is lucky to take three or four shots on goal in an entire game.

Shooting is an art that must be learned during practice. Every player should practice five basic shots, each demanding accuracy, balance, and power. These skills, more than any others, will help a young hockey player get the most out of every shot.

The wrist shot, or forehand shot, is the most common—and probably the most accurate shot a player can make. It starts with a sweeping motion that allows a shooter to line up the shot. It ends with a snap of the wrist, giving the puck speed and power.

A wrist shot is taken by sweeping, or pushing, the blade forward using the bottom hand on the shaft. You shoot with the inside, or curved side, of the blade. Many coaches insist that players perfect the wrist shot, even at the expense of other shots.

When practicing the wrist shot, you should follow through with the stick towards the intended target, similar to the way a golfer, or batter in baseball, follows through at the end of a stroke or swing.

The snap shot is also a type of forehand shot. It is like the wrist shot but without the sweeping motion. The snap shot is not as fast or accurate as the wrist shot, but it is often a better choice because it does not give the defense any warning that you are about to take a shot. And that can give your team an advantage.

★ **DID YOU KNOW?**

Sticks have different degrees of stiffness, or flexibility. Players who favor the wrist shot will most likely choose a flexible stick. Players who have powerful wind-ups and make frequent slap shots will choose a stiffer stick.

An instructor demonstrates a slap shot.

Hockey coaches instruct players on how to shoot.

A slap shot is the fastest shot a player can use. Some **professional** players can slap shot a puck over 100 miles an hour. A puck traveling at such high speed has a chance of scoring no matter how quick the goalkeeper is. Slap shots, however, are not usually a player's first choice, because slap shots are generally not very accurate.

To take a slap shot, you should stand with your feet at least shoulder width apart. Raise your stick to waist level or higher. As you bring the stick down, shift your weight from your back leg to the front leg. This will put force into the shot. Also, as you bring the stick down, aim the blade just behind the puck, hitting the ice. The force in the shot will cause the shaft of the stick to bend slightly, which adds power as you follow-through and make contact with the puck.

★ COACH'S CORNER

A goalie wears a blocker glove on the stick hand and a catcher glove on the other hand. If you aim the puck low and close to the stick, the goalie can't catch the puck.

The flip shot is the best choice for sending the puck into the high corners of the goal. The flip shot can be used to pop the puck up and over or between obstacles like a player or a player's stick. This shot is good for shooting a rebound close to the net.

The flip shot is fun and easy to practice. Using the front, or toe, of the blade, scoop the puck up and quickly flip your wrists forward. Practice the flip shot by aiming at an obstacle on the ice.

A backhand shot requires a pulling motion of your lower hand rather than the pushing motion used in a forehand shot. The backhand shot is more difficult than it was before sticks had curved blades. A backhand shot, used less often than other shots, often catches the goalkeeper off guard.

A coach shows how to follow-through.

Players practice shots on goal.

A backhand shot is performed using the back side of the blade, close to the heel. Use your lower hand to pull the stick and sweep the puck towards the goal. Your top hand is used for control. Be careful not to flip your wrists too much, sending the puck too high.

Remember, your position when you shoot is critical to the effectiveness of your shot. An attempt from the **slot** (the area in front of the goal) is much more likely to score than a shot from anywhere else on the ice. When facing the goal straight on, you see its entire six foot (almost 2 meters) width. The goalie has to protect that entire area. However, when shooting from outside of the slot, on either the far right or far left side, the puck will approach the goal at an angle. The target (goal) looks much smaller from here. And the goalie has a smaller area to protect. This is why your shot is harder to make.

Don't be afraid to pass the puck or try to move into a better scoring position before attempting a shot on goal.

CHAPTER THREE

FACE-OFF

Good hockey players must be excellent skaters, but more importantly they must be team players. Learning to play well together takes time and a lot of hard work for a group of players. Knowing how your teammates will react in any situation will give your team an advantage over your opponent.

A Basic Play

As with any sport, hockey involves basic **strategies** that all players have to master. A face-off is one of the most basic plays. In a face-off, an **official** drops the puck between the sticks of two opposing players.

The two players stand with their shoulders square to each other, each player facing the opponent's end of the rink. Both players rest their sticks on the ice and wait for the official to drop the puck. They focus on the puck in the official's hand. The official looks to make sure no other player is within 15 feet (about 4 1/2 meters) of the face-off spot and that no one is offside. The official then drops the puck, flat side down, and the game begins. If you win the face off, your team goes on the **offense**. If you lose, your team goes on the **defense**.

A face-off is often held in one of five face-off circles painted on the rink. One face-off circle is in the center of the rink. Two more can be found in each **defensive zone**. Four more face-off spots are near the blue lines in the **neutral zone**.

A face-off occurs many times during a game. Each period starts with a face-off at center ice. The puck is dropped by the official. The two opposing players fight for control of the puck; then, pass it to a teammate to begin setting up for a play.

★ **COACH'S CORNER**

Guarding the goal is the first priority when taking a face-off in your defensive zone.

22

This face-off occurs at a face-off spot in the neutral zone.

Knocking the opponent's stick aside may give you time to scoop the puck in the direction of a teammate.

A face-off also takes place after a goal is scored and when play has been stopped by an official. If play is stopped by an official, the face-off occurs near the spot where the puck was last in play.

The face-off is an important part of any hockey game. A face-off can occur as many as 70 times in a typical game. A team that wins the face-off battle most often has more opportunities to score goals and therefore has a good chance to win more games.

Most often the center is the player who takes the face-off. When taking a face-off a player squares off against the opponent, feet wide apart for balance and power. The stick should be positioned on the ice over the face-off dot. One hand should be high on the stick while the other grips the stick just above the blade. This position offers the best combination of control and power. It is important to know where your teammates are so that you can scoop the puck in their direction. When an official drops the puck, a quick response and good strategy will help you win the face-off.

★ DID YOU KNOW?

Your team should have a strategy for every face-off. Every team member should know exactly what the plan is and each player's responsibility, whether you win or lose the face-off.

Winning the Face-Off

A winning face-off play begins before the actual face-off occurs. To win a face-off, start by studying the position of your opponent just before the face-off. The opposing center may give you clues about his or her plan. Look to see how the body and stick are positioned. Watch for eye contact between the center and his or her teammates. You may notice that the center always looks toward the teammate intended to get the pass. When the puck is about to be dropped, shift your eyes from your opponent to the official. Focus on the puck in the official's hand. Be ready to react the instant the puck is dropped.

A game begins with a face-off at center ice.

A team that wins the most face-offs will have more opportunities to score goals.

There are many techniques for winning a face-off. The most common way is to knock your opponent's stick aside as the official drops the puck. This action may give you just enough time to scoop the puck in the direction of a teammate. However, since this technique is so common, your opponent probably will be expecting it. In fact, your opponent may attempt the same technique on you! For this reason you need to have more than one strategy. Watch your opponent closely each time you face off. You may discover that your opponent uses the same techniques over and over. The more you learn about your opponent the more success you will have in face-offs. Experience is your best teacher.

OFFENSE

Offense means "attack" and it's a good way to describe what happens when a hockey team gains possession of the puck. A hockey team can go on the offense any place on the ice. When a team wins a face-off or steals the puck from the opposing team they become the offense. Hockey is a fast-paced game and a team must be able to switch back and forth from offense to defense in the blink of an eye.

Defensive Zone

A **breakout** is one of the most exciting plays in hockey. A breakout usually occurs when a team's defense player (left or right) takes possession of the puck in the defense zone. Breakout plays are designed to get the puck from the defensive zone into scoring position.

The defense has several options, depending on where the puck is intercepted, or taken. If the defense player is a good skater and has open ice in front, he or she may choose to take the puck up the ice into the neutral zone. If the defense player is a very good skater and has the opportunity, he or she may take the puck all the way to the **attack zone**. In this case, a winger will need to drop back to cover the defense position.

A more common breakout play has the defense players passing the puck to one of the forwards (left wing, center, or right wing) who will take the puck up the ice.

Once a team breaks out of its defensive zone and enters the neutral zone, they need to set up their next play. The position of the opponents helps a team know which play to use from the hundreds of possibilities.

★ **COACH'S CORNER**

Some coaches, as a last resort, will replace the goalie with a forward in the remaining minutes of a losing game. This strategy is risky, but teams that use it sometimes come from behind and win the game. This is referred to as "pulling the goalie."

Offensive skills include good stickhandling.

The goalie is in position to block the shot.

Many times the player in control of the puck will be forechecked by two or even three opponents. This is a good opportunity to pass the puck to an open teammate, who can take a shot at the goal or pass the puck to a third teammate.

Attacking Zone

Hockey is a game of percentages, meaning that the more shots on goal a team has the more likely they are to score. At the same time, it is important to take shots that are most likely to score a goal.

Shots taken from 10 feet to 25 feet (3 to 7 1/2 meters) in front of the goal most often result in a goal. This scoring zone is called the slot. A successful team tries to have at least one player in the slot at all times during an offensive play. Not all goals are scored from the slot, though. A goal scored from elsewhere on the ice is just as valuable.

A player lined up in the slot is also in good position to rebound a missed shot. A rebound shot may result in a goal more often than an original shot because the goalkeeper may have moved out of position.

★ **DID YOU KNOW?**

A good team can score on 20 percent of their power plays. Power plays often determine the winner of a game.

The Power Play

A **power play** occurs when an opposing team loses one or two players due to **penalties**. The player or players who draw a penalty are sent to the penalty box giving the other team a temporary player advantage. The team with more players is said to be "on the power play."

The key to a successful power play is puck control. A team on a power play will sometimes commit an extra player to an attack. In fact, some coaches replace one of the defense players with an extra forward. The extra forward increases passing opportunities and keeps the opposing team on the run.

A defenseman breaks out into the neutral zone.

Players rush to gain control of the puck.

A power play called "the spread" takes advantage of a team's superior numbers. The team on the power play spreads out across the attack zone, forcing the opposing defense to defend a larger area. Then the puck is passed back and forth until an opportunity to make a shot opens up. The spread is an effective play, but it's also risky because it leaves your defensive zone open to attack if you should lose control of the puck. The defense players and the wings must be ready to drop back quickly if control of the puck is lost.

If the team on the power play scores a goal, the player in the penalty box is now allowed back into the game. Both teams are with even number players again or "even strength."

DEFENSE

Just as a hockey team becomes the offense when they gain possession of the puck, they also become the defense the instant they lose control of the puck.

Defense is not the responsibility of just the left and right defense players and the goalkeeper. Defense is a team effort.

Being "on the defense" means trying to keep the other team from scoring a goal *and* to regain possession of the puck. Once the puck is back in your control, you are back on the offense. The more time your team spends on offense the more opportunities you have to score goals.

Checking is a defensive skill used to slow down or stop the player who has possession of the puck. **Forechecking** is an important skill for any hockey player to learn. Forechecking involves going after the offensive player, who has possession of the puck, before that player breaks out of the defensive zone. If a forecheck is successful, a team may be able to recover the puck while in their attack zone. A forecheck at least slows down the opponent's breakout. Checking can be done using the body (body-check) or the stick (stick-check).

Body-checking makes hockey a contact sport. A legal body-check can be used only against the player who has the puck. (Note: Body-checking is not allowed currently in women's hockey). A player may use only the trunk of the body (the hips to the shoulders) to check an opponent. Use of the limbs or head to check an opponent results in a penalty. A player also may be penalized for **charging** if he or she rushes and checks an opponent from more than two strides away.

★ **DID YOU KNOW?**

A team is shorthanded when they have fewer players on the ice due to penalties. They bring in "penalty killers," players who specialize in defense. A team's penalty killing strategy is meant to keep the opponent from scoring.

The goalie is the last line of defense.

Players scramble for the puck along the boards.

The most common body-check is the shoulder-check. To throw a shoulder-check, you should stay low, bend your knees, keep your head up, and using the shoulder nearest your opponent, aim at the chest. If you stand too tall when throwing a shoulder-check, you may be the one that ends up sprawled on the ice. An effective shoulder check pins the opponent on the boards (wall of the rink) or may take him or her out of play.

Another type of body-check is known as the hip-check. One effective way to throw a hip-check is to bend over at the waist, standing sideways in the path of your opponent. You need to do this at the last possible moment so your opponent does not have time to change direction. The opponent will fall over you and lose control of the puck. A hip-check is not easy to pull off. It should be attempted only when the odds of success are high.

Stick-checking is the most-used method of stealing the puck from an opponent. A stick can be used many ways in checking. The most successful method is called "poke-checking." In a poke-check, you simply use your stick blade to poke at your opponent's stick or at the puck.

41

If your opponent is caught off guard, the puck can be knocked away. The problem with poke-checking is that in knocking the puck away, you also lose control of the puck yourself. Still, poke-checking is good for breaking up an opponent's play and possibly opening an opportunity for your team to take the puck.

Hook-checking is another stick-check method. With the blade of your stick lying flat on the ice, you reach for the puck, hook it, and pull it away from your opponent.

Opposing players practice puck control drills.

The goalie takes a defensive stance as the attacking player attempts a shot on goal.

A sweep-check occurs when a player lays his or her stick on the ice, holding it with one hand. The player then makes a sweeping motion towards the puck, trying to knock it away from the opponent. The player may gain possession of the puck or at least knock it into a teammate's reach.

Illegal checking will result in a minor penalty where the player committing the infraction is ruled off the ice for 2 minutes. Any action by the players with the intent to injure can result in a misconduct penalty and possibly ejection from the game. Other misconducts and penalties are discussed in *Rules of the Game*—another book in this series.

GLOSSARY

attack zone (uh TAK ZON) — area on the ice between opponent's blue line and goal line

blade (BLAYD) — the bottom section of the stick between the heel (back) and the toe (front)

body-checking (BAHD ee CHEK ing) — using the hips or shoulders to throw off an opponent who is in possession of the puck

breakout (BRAYK OUT) — play used by an attacking team to move the puck out of their defensive zone toward the opponent's goal

charging (CHAHRG ing) — taking two or more steps or strides to check an opponent

checking (CHEK ing) — using your body or stick to slow down or stop an opponent in possession of the puck

defense (DEE fens) — team trying to gain possession of the puck; also, plays to keep the opponent from scoring; player positions (left and right) on a hockey team

defensive zone (di FEN siv ZON) — area on the ice between the blue line and your team's goal line

forechecking (FAWR CHEK ing) — covering an opponent in your offensive zone to prevent an attack

neutral zone (NOO trul ZON) — area on the ice between the two blue lines, also called "center ice"

offense (AHF ens) — team in control of the puck; the attacking team

GLOSSARY

official (uh FISH ul) — person trained in hockey rules who supervises some part of games, such as (on ice) *referee*, who calls rule violations and imposes penalties, and *linesman* who calls rule infractions; also (off-ice) goal *judges*, *penalty timekeeper*, *game timekeeper*, and *scorer*.

opponent (uh PO nent) — player on the other team

penalties (PEN ul teez) — punishments for breaking hockey rules

power play (POW er PLAY) — when a team that outnumbers its opponent on the ice tries to score a goal

professional (pruh FESH uh nul) — someone paid to participate in a sport

shaft (SHAFT) — the long midsection of a hockey stick

slot (SLAHT)— best scoring area on the ice, between the two face-off circles

stickhandling (STIK HAN dling) — guiding a puck with a hockey stick

strategies (STRAT eh jeez) — plans of action to gain a specific advantage over an opponent

FURTHER READING

Find out more with these helpful books and information sites:

Harris, Lisa. *Hockey How to Play the All-Star Way.* Austin, TX: Raintree Steck-Vaughn Publishers. 1994

Davidson, John, with John Steinbreder. *Hockey for Dummies An Official Publication of the NHL.* IDG Books Worldwide, Inc. 1997

Canadian Hockey Association at www.canadianhockey.ca/

International Ice Hockey Federation (IIHF) at www.iihf.com

National Hockey League at www.nhl.com

USA Hockey, Inc. at www.usahockey.com

INDEX